PIANO SOLO

A **STEVEN SPIELBERG** FILM

THE FABELMANS

WRITTEN BY S T E V E N   S P I E L B E R G & T O N Y   K U S H N E R

MUSIC FROM THE ORIGINAL MOTION PICTURE SOUNDTRACK

ORIGINAL MUSIC COMPOSED BY J O H N   W I L L I A M S

ISBN 978-1-70518-758-6

Visit Hal Leonard Online at
www.halleonard.com

World headquarters, contact:
Hal Leonard
7777 West Bluemound Road
Milwaukee, WI 53213
Email: info@halleonard.com

In Europe, contact:
Hal Leonard Europe Limited
1 Red Place
London, W1K 6PL
Email: info@halleonardeurope.com

In Australia, contact:
Hal Leonard Australia Pty. Ltd.
4 Lentara Court
Cheltenham, Victoria, 3192 Australia
Email: info@halleonard.com.au

THE FABELMANS

By JOHN WILLIAMS

Moderately, flowing

teneramente

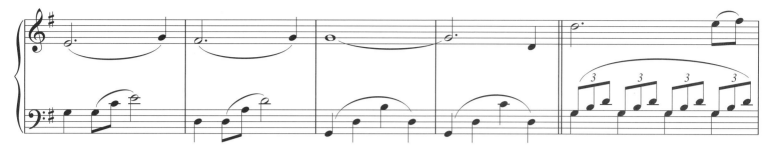

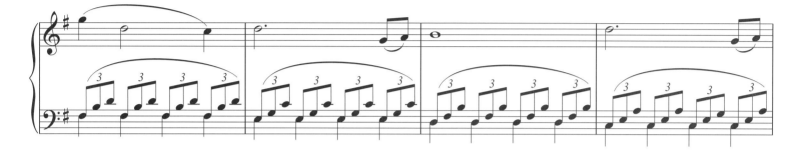

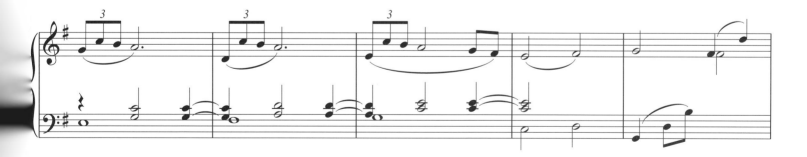

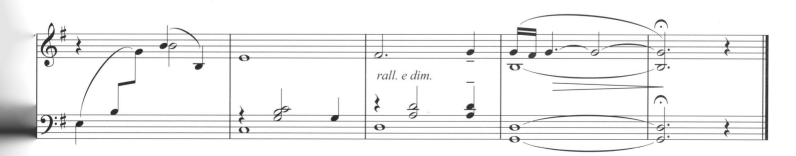

rall. e dim.

MITZI'S DANCE

By JOHN WILLIAMS

Moderately slow

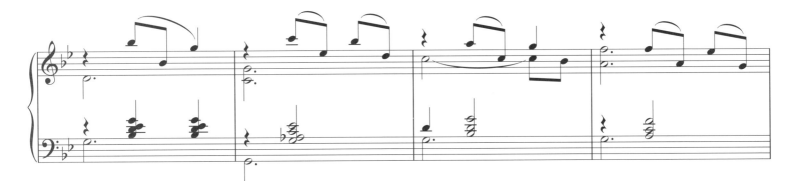

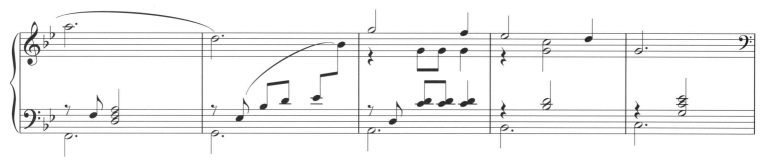

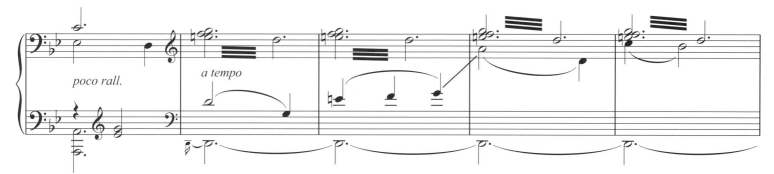

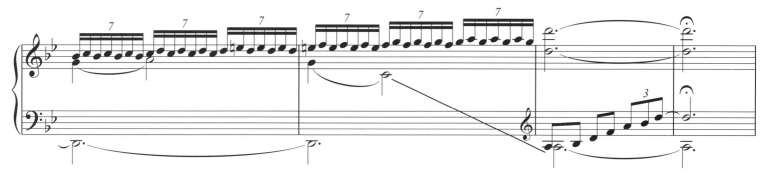

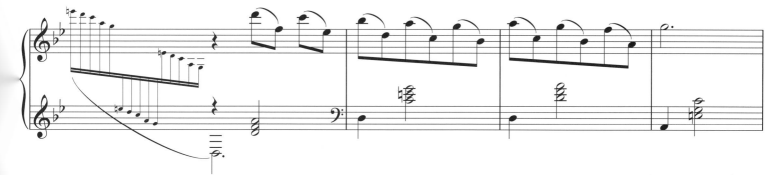

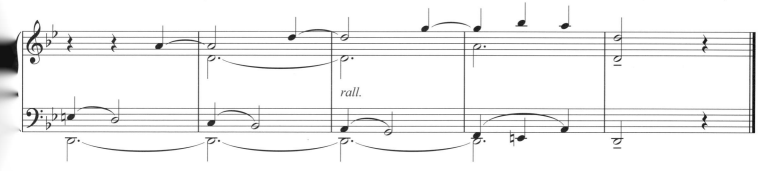

REVERIE

By JOHN WILLIAMS

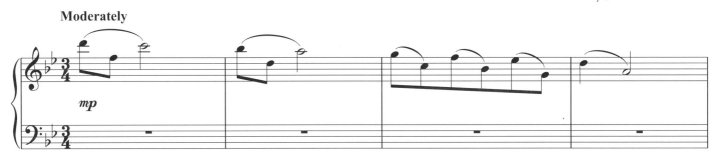

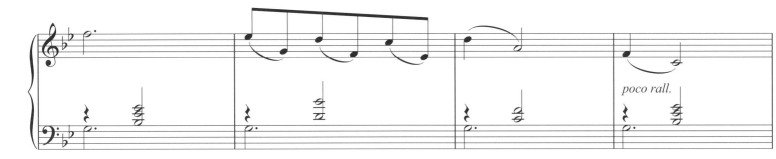

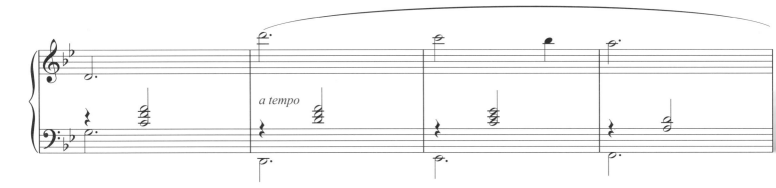

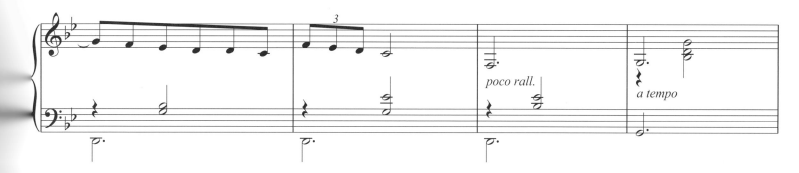

MOTHER AND SON

By JOHN WILLIAMS

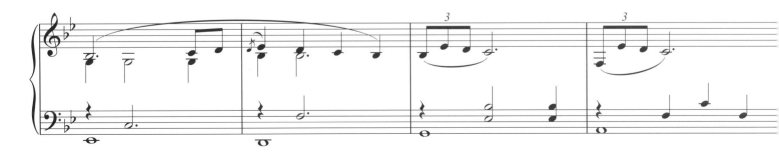

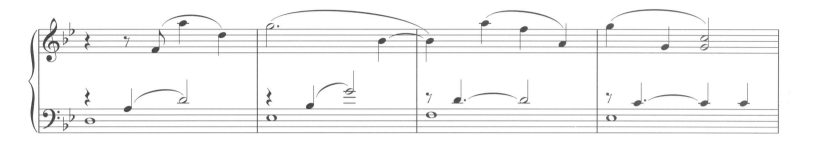

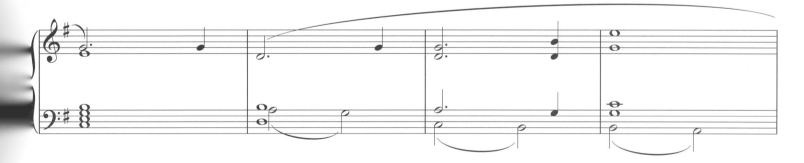

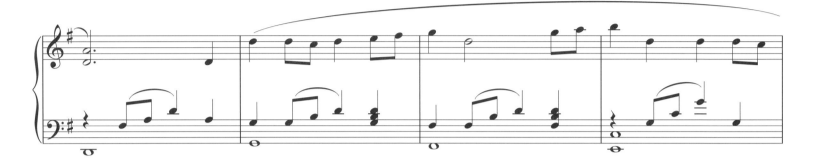

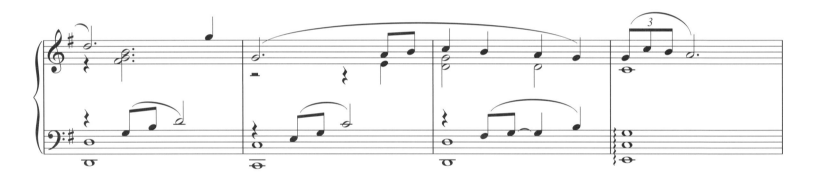

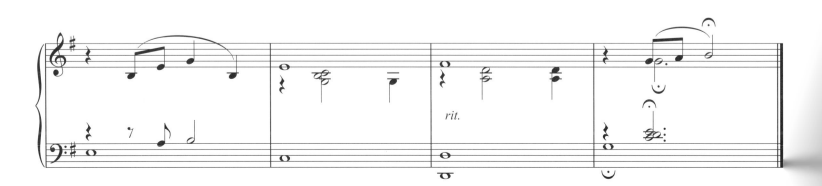

SONATINA IN C MAJOR
Op. 36, No. 3: Spiritoso

Music by MUZIO CLEMENTI

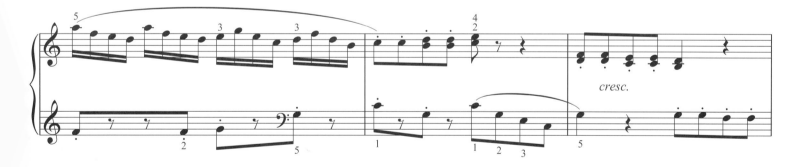

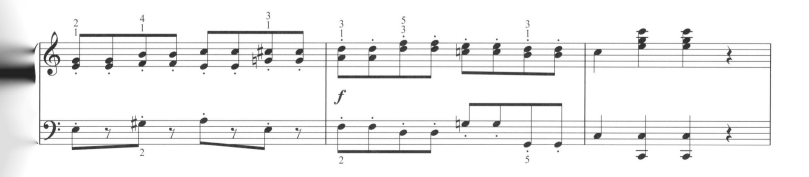

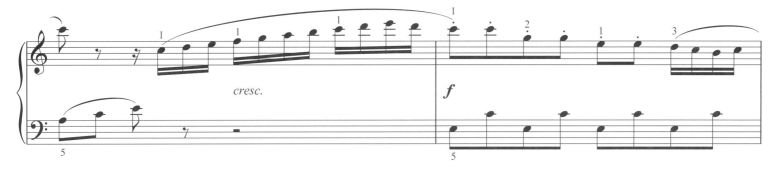

REFLECTIONS

By JOHN WILLIAMS

Moderately, expressively

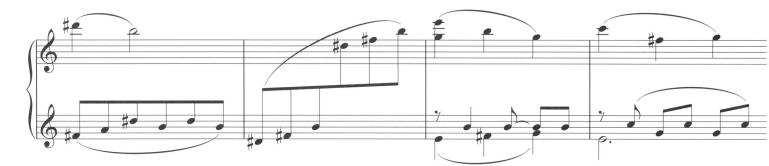

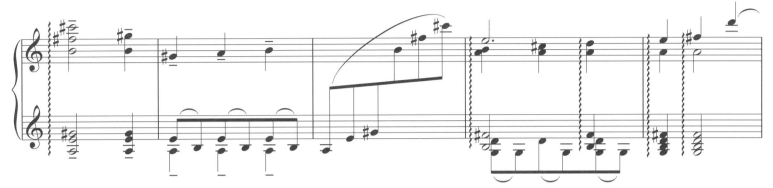

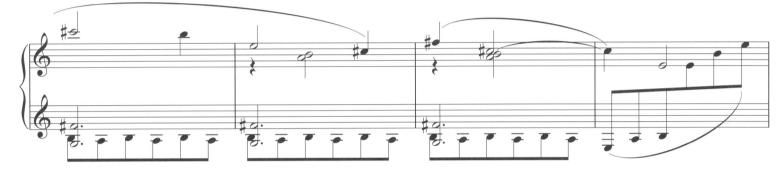

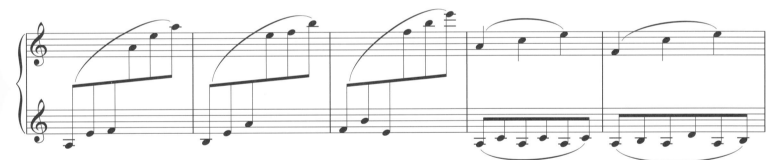

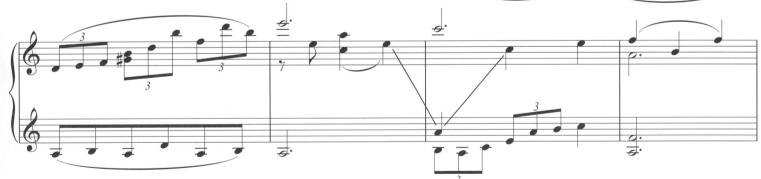

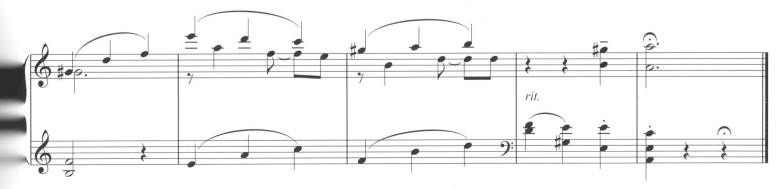

rit.

THE LETTER

By JOHN WILLIAMS

Moderately slow

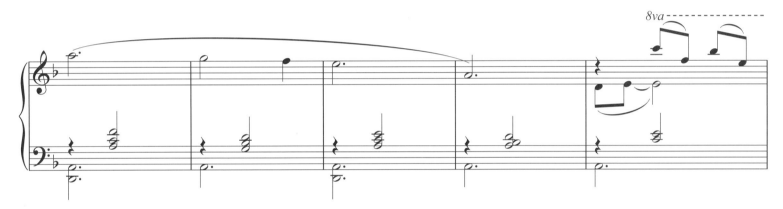

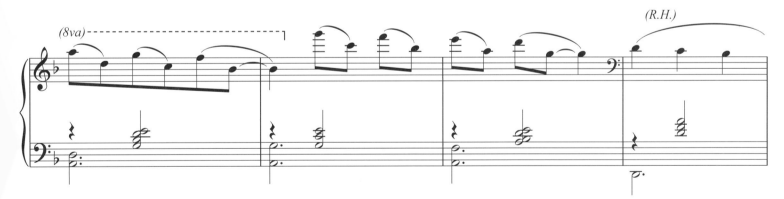

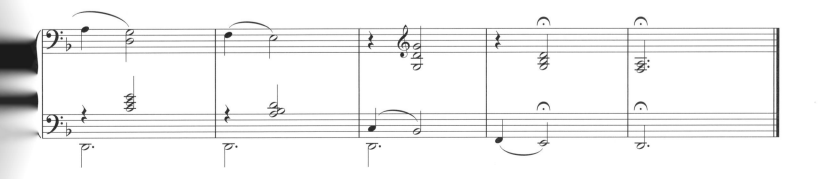

SONATINA IN A MINOR
Op. 88, No. 3
III. Allegro burlesco

Music by FRIEDRICH KUHLAU

Allegro burlesco [♩ = ca. 132]

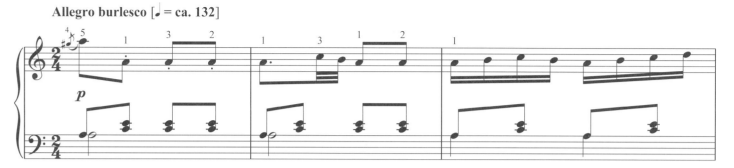

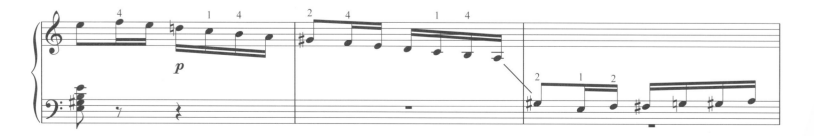

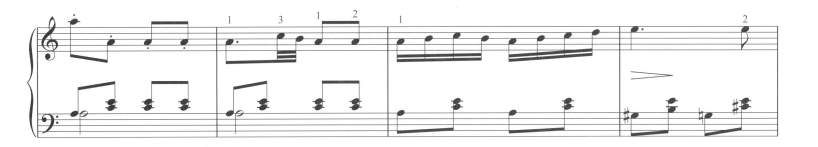

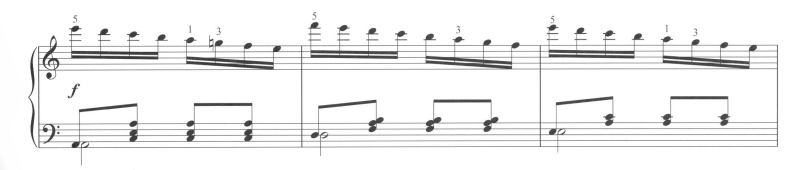

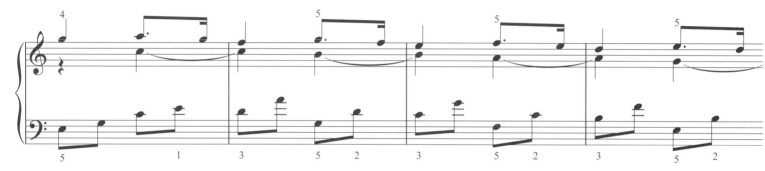

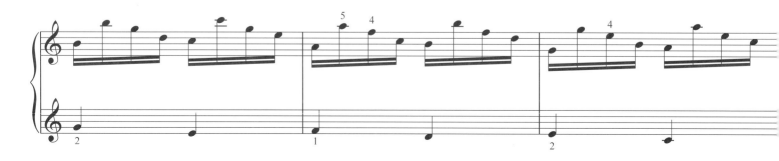

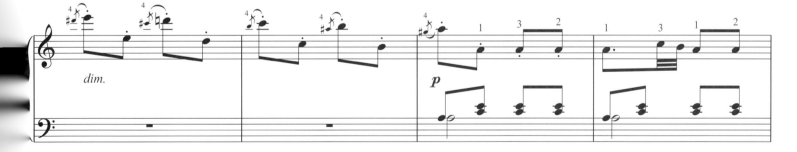

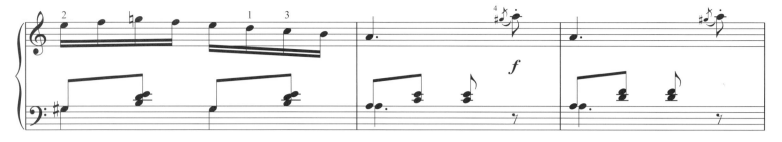

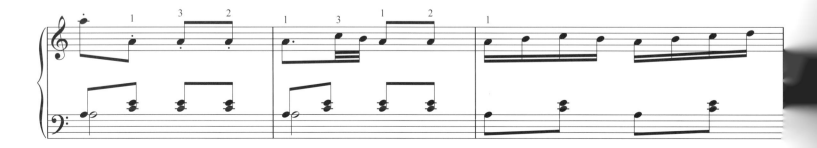

CONCERTO IN D MINOR, BWV 974
II. Adagio

Music by ALESSANDRO MARCELLO
Transcribed by J.S. BACH

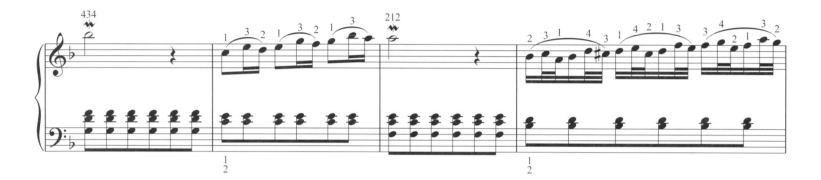

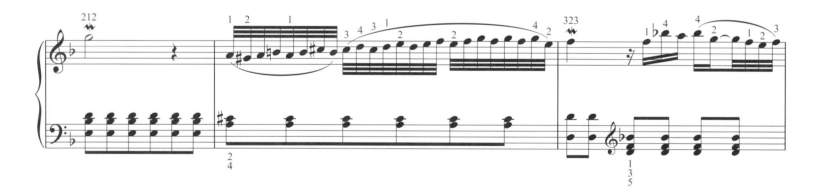

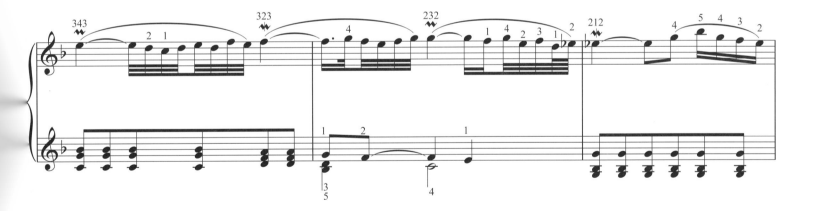

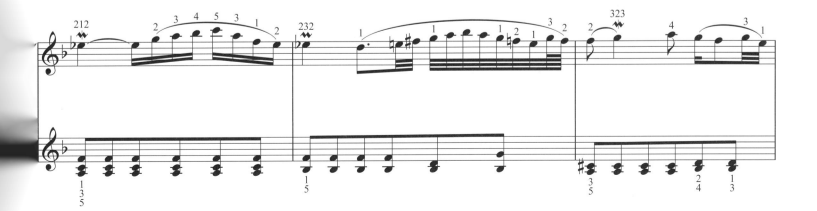

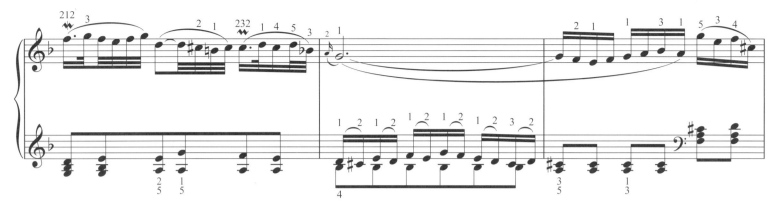

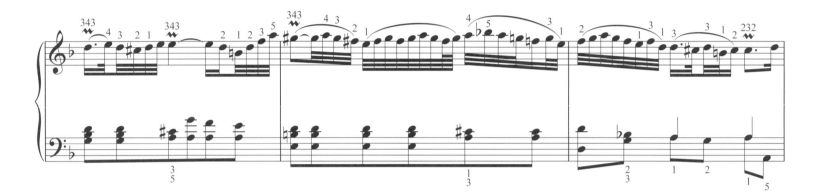

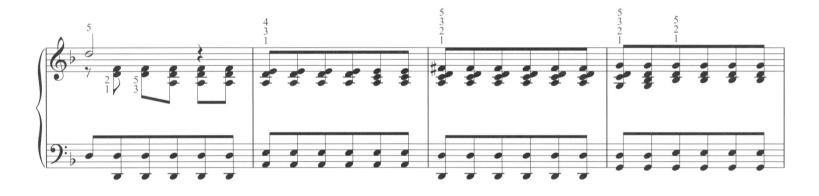

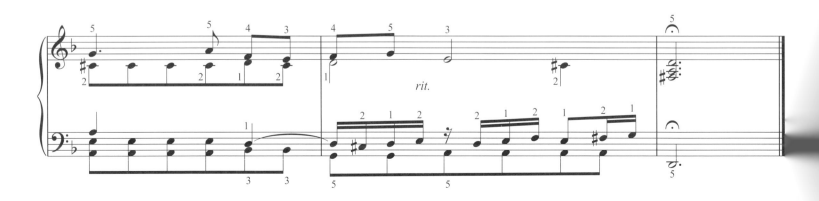